EXPLORING THE WORLD OF
Raccoons

Tracy C. Read

FIREFLY BOOKS

A FIREFLY BOOK

Published by Firefly Books Ltd. 2010

First Printing

Publisher Cataloging-in-Publication Data (U.S.)
Read, Tracy C.
    Raccoons / Tracy C. Read.
[ ] p. : col. photos. ; cm.
Exploring the world of.
Includes index.
ISBN-13: 978-1-55407-626-0 (bound)
ISBN-10: 1-55407-626-9 (bound)
ISBN-13: 978-1-55407-617-8 (pbk.)
ISBN-10: 1-55407-617-X (pbk.)
1. Raccoons - Juvenile literature.
I. Exploring the world of. II. Title.
599.74443 dc22   QL737.C26R434 2010

Library and Archives Canada
   Cataloguing in Publication
Read, Tracy C.
    Exploring the world of raccoons /
   Tracy C. Read.
Includes index.
ISBN-13: 978-1-55407-617-8 (pbk.)
ISBN-10: 1-55407-617-X (pbk.)
ISBN-13: 978-1-55407-626-0 (bound)
ISBN-10: 1-55407-626-9 (bound)
1. Raccoon--Juvenile literature. I. Title
QL737.C26R42 2009
j599.76'32   C2009-905117-6

Published in the United States by
Firefly Books (U.S.) Inc.
P.O. Box 1338, Ellicott Station
Buffalo, New York 14205

Published in Canada by
Firefly Books Ltd.
66 Leek Crescent
Richmond Hill, Ontario L4B 1H1

The Publisher gratefully acknowledges the financial support for our publishing program by the Government of Canada through the Canada Book Fund as administered by the Department of Canadian Heritage.

Cover and interior design by
Janice McLean, Bookmakers Press Inc.
jmclean14@cogeco.ca

Manufactured by Printplus Limited in Shen Zhen, Guang Dong, P.R.China in December, 2009, Job #S091100068

CONTENTS

ESCAPE ARTIST
Sturdy but agile, the raccoon has mastered the art of getting into and out of confined spaces.

MEET THE RACCOON

With its signature black bandit's mask and ringed tail, the common raccoon (*Procyon lotor*) is a familiar figure. In fact, city dwellers are probably as likely to come face-to-face with this medium-sized mammal in their darkened driveways as are hikers and campers to spot it in the wild. When we do, the raccoon rarely scampers off in fright. Instead, it stands its ground, at least for a few moments, as if to signal that it has just as much right to be here as we do.

Indeed, it does, if its ability to adapt to new circumstances is a good measuring stick. Facing the loss of its North American forest habitat in the early 20th century, where it traditionally lived near wetlands, the common raccoon began to make its move to the suburbs and then to the downtown core of cities, large and small. Today, whether we find its presence charming or maddening, the raccoon lives among us, sometimes literally — in our garages, chimneys, attics and basements.

The word "raccoon" comes from the word *arathcone*, Algonquian for "one who scratches with his hands." As we'll learn, the raccoon's dexterity with its handlike forepaws is just one of the many strengths this stocky little critter exploits to survive. Whether in its native habitat or living among humans, the raccoon brings intelligence and problem-solving skills to every aspect of its daily life.

ANATOMY LESSON

The short, sturdy raccoon has a ringed tail, rounded ears, a pointed snout and a distinctive black mask that stands out against the pale gray fur above its eyes and on its muzzle. Its long salt-and-pepper coat has tones of black, brown and gray. Coarse guard hairs help shed moisture, while a dense undercoat provides insulation. The raccoon's underbelly fur is brownish white.

One biologist compares the size of an average raccoon to that of a fat cat, and some are fatter than others. Weights range from 12 to 30 pounds (5.4-13.6 kg), and the male is typically larger than the female.

With its short legs, the raccoon is not the fastest animal in the forest, but it can accelerate up to 15 miles per hour (24 kph) over short distances. To run down trees headfirst, it rotates its hind feet 180 degrees. It's a formidable opponent when cornered and is also a strong swimmer.

Another notable feature is the raccoon's paws. Both front and back paws have five flexible fingerlike digits, each with a sharp, nonretractable claw. Standing on its hind legs, it can use its front paws to examine and manipulate food or other objects of interest.

Not to be discounted is the raccoon's intelligence and its remarkable memory, which, in combination with its physical strengths, make this wild creature a force to be reckoned with.

LOOKS & BRAINS

The raccoon's mischievous masked face has great appeal. Not quite so cute is its talent for opening doors, latches and garbage bins.

RACCOON FACTS

Special features
Black face mask, ringed tail and dexterous front paws

Average lifespan in the wild
More than 4 years

Diet
Omnivore

Offspring
1 to 7 (typically 3 or 4) per litter; 1 litter per year

Weight
12 to 30 pounds (5.4-13.6 kg) and up to 55 pounds (25 kg) Many subspecies of raccoon are found in North America; northern residents are typically heavier.

Raccoon in motion
An expert climber, the raccoon can reach speeds of up to 15 miles per hour (24 kph) on the ground.

Tail length
8½ to 10 inches (22-25 cm)

Total length
2½ to 3 feet (0.8-0.9 m)

HANG IN THERE

Remarkably agile, the compact raccoon uses its handlike paws to climb trees and scramble into small spaces.

IT'S ALL IN THE DETAILS

The raccoon's black mask may reduce glare and boost its night vision, while its large nose sniffs out food and foes. The coarse guard hairs on the raccoon's coat are moisture-resistant, and a protective layer of skin on its paws becomes extra-sensitive when wet.

NATURAL TALENTS

As animals navigate their world, they depend on all five senses — touch, taste, hearing, sight and smell — to stay safe and healthy. For the raccoon, a well-developed sense of touch is at the center of its success. In fact, according to researchers, a large portion of the raccoon's cerebral cortex (the brain's "gray matter") is devoted to touch.

Hypersensitive paws help the raccoon learn about its surroundings, and its fingerlike digits (including a flexible "thumb") allow it to handle and access a vast range of foods, from clams and nuts to the organic material in your garbage can or composter.

The natural consequence of this ability is that the raccoon has developed a taste for virtually every food group found in its range. An omnivore, it eats both animal and plant matter.

The raccoon's ears can detect tones in both the lower and the upper registers. It is able to hear sounds as subtle as an earthworm burrowing through the soil as well as the shrill communication calls from other raccoons or the approach of a potential predator.

For a night-active mammal, night vision is a must. The raccoon can distinguish shapes in different lighting situations, though it does not have good long-distance vision.

Last, but not least, the raccoon's sense of smell enables it to follow the scent trail of its fellow raccoons.

GREAT HANDS
The raccoon's handlike paws are key to its success.

TOUCH
Manual dexterity increases the raccoon's feeding opportunities.

HEARING
The raccoon's ears are sensitive to high and low sound frequencies.

SIGHT
Good night vision is important for an animal that hunts after dark.

TASTE
The complete menu of raccoon foods features thousands of items.

SMELL
Leaving a strong-smelling scent trail allows raccoons to stay connected.

MAKING A LIVING

The common raccoon belongs to the Procyonidae family, a group of dog-sized animals that, for the most part, make their home in the warmer climes of South and Central America, Mexico and the southern United States. Some 2½ million years ago, however, the raccoon, along with several other southern mammals, made its way northward to a more temperate environment. Today, it is comfortably established throughout most of the United States and southern Canada. Populations of raccoons also exist in Europe and Asia, but these were introduced by humans.

To survive, the raccoon must have access to fresh water, an adequate supply of food and a safe place to make a den. The intelligent, highly adaptive North American raccoon seems to have little trouble satisfying its needs over a wide range of habitats. It can be found along oceans, rivers and streams, in marshland, prairies and forests and even in suburbs and cities. The only real estate options the raccoon doesn't find appealing are areas where the winters are long and harsh and regions at high altitude, where water sources can freeze even in summer.

Like all successful animals, the raccoon is able to adjust to changing circumstances. In the wild, it makes its den near water, whether in a hollow tree, a protected rock crevice, an abandoned animal

BEG, BORROW OR STEAL

At an early age, the raccoon learns how to exploit its feeding opportunities, whether "dabbling" in a stream for fish or pleading with its human neighbors for a small handout.

WHAT'S ON THE MENU?

An omnivore, the raccoon will chow down on whatever is available, from corn, fruits and nuts to insects, frogs and fish.

burrow or a pile of brush. In the city, it invades buildings, setting up house in attics, sheds, garages, basements and warehouses.

One of the world's most accomplished omnivores, the raccoon eats animal and plant matter of all descriptions. Its diet varies throughout the year, depending on the season, and it displays at least two notable eating styles. With dry foods, such as nuts, the raccoon stands on its hind legs and rubs and rolls the food in its paws. When fishing, it uses a technique called "dousing" or "dabbling," conducting a thorough underwater search for prey using its handlike paws, which become extra-sensitive when wet. One researcher describes the raccoon as gazing off into space while it explores its food through touch. (Today, scientists agree that raccoons in the wild do not "wash" their food, though captive raccoons may instinctively perform a look-alike action.)

This nighttime forager makes a meal of insects and worms, crayfish, eggs, birds, fruit, nuts, carrion, corn and other vegetable material. In human communities, it raids garbage cans, pet food dishes, bird feeders and backyard gardens. Wherever it ventures, the forward-thinking raccoon appears to have cracked the code for successful living.

COATI COUSINS

A procyonid relative of the raccoon, the coati makes its home in Central and South America, Mexico and the southern United States.

TREE FORT

A popular den choice for a mother raccoon is a hollow tree, where her young family is safely off the ground.

STAYING ALIVE

In late summer and autumn, raccoons start to pack on the pounds. Some gain more than an extra inch of insulating fat before bedding down in a den to sleep away the long, cold months. A hard winter can be tough on a raccoon population. Young raccoons and unhealthy or injured adults are especially vulnerable. Inevitably, some die from exposure or starvation. Year-round, raccoons are also prone to disease and infection, including rabies, distemper and roundworm.

Just as the raccoon regards almost anything as a potential meal, there is a long list of fellow creatures in the wild ready to call the raccoon dinner. However, with its muscular build, sharp teeth and impressive tree-climbing talent, a night-active adult raccoon isn't an easy target. Its young, on the other hand, are less able to defend themselves. Cougars, bobcats, foxes, coyotes, fishers, wolves and even great horned owls hunt the raccoon.

But humans are by far the raccoon's greatest enemy. For centuries, North Americans have hunted and trapped the raccoon for its fur and meat. Farmers whose crops and chickens have been ravaged by raccoons often eliminate these pesky marauders. And the raccoon carnage strewn along our back roads and highways is a gruesome reminder of what happens when cars and raccoons cross paths after dark.

WATCH YOUR BACK

Large carnivores and raptors (including the fisher, lynx, owl and wolf) prey on the raccoon in the wild, though declining predator populations make that less of a danger. Humans pose a much greater threat to the raccoon.

16

PLAYING HOUSE

When the temperature starts to rise and the days grow longer, the raccoon rouses itself from its seasonal slumber (it sleeps rather than hibernates in the winter) and emerges from its den to resume an active life. The male, or boar, roams its territory in search of a female, or sow, often finding one or more at a central meeting place in early spring.

After mating with a female, however, the male's contribution to the next generation is finished. Some two months later, in an existing den or a new den, the female gives birth to a litter of anywhere from one to seven kits.

The kits are blind and helpless at birth. Within two to three weeks, their eyes open, but their eyesight takes longer to develop.

BABY LOVE

Making a low purring sound, a raccoon mother gathers her young, which cry when hungry or lonely.

After about 10 days, their little face masks begin to stand out.

Solely responsible for family life, the female nurses her young for roughly 14 weeks, although the kits also eat bits of solid food before they are weaned. At two months, they venture outside the den on their own or with their siblings, displaying the raccoon's trademark curiosity about all things. As they play and explore their surroundings, the kits fine-tune the skills they will need to survive on their own.

In late spring and early summer, the mother guides the kits on foraging trips to nearby creeks, streams and fields and teaches them to hunt, climb and swim.

Some of the juvenile raccoons leave during the fall to establish their own territories. While the young females stick close to their mother's home range, the males travel farther afield. Families may den together through the winter but separate in the spring when the adult female gives birth to her next litter.

RACCOON WALKABOUT
A raccoon family carefully combs the forest floor to find food.

THE FAMILY BUSINESS
Raccoons seem to understand the theory of locking mechanisms. This raccoon kit is learning the tricks of the trade from its mother.

WILD ON THE STREET

Whether we like it or not, city-loving raccoons are a human legacy. Over the past century, as rural North Americans migrated to urban centers, raccoons followed. Driven from wetlands and woodlands as cities and towns swallowed up their habitats, raccoons quickly discovered the benefits of living close to ready accommodation and easy food.

In the city, humans and raccoons have little choice but to coexist, even if we humans are a little uneasy about it. By night, we hear their snarls and cries as they fight for food or mates or territory. We watch with amusement as a mother leads her kits through the streets or up a tree at dusk. We clean up the mess when they raid our garbage bins. And when these masked mammals make themselves at home in our houses and garages, we usually evict them humanely, even though their architectural alterations may cost us thousands to repair.

But raccoons make sacrifices to live in the city, just as we do. Population density brings competition for food and living spaces. It also creates a breeding ground for diseases that may pose a threat to humans — and can cause a slow, agonizing death for the raccoon.

So although we tolerate these little Houdinis, it's in our best interest and theirs to thwart their inclination to overtake our spaces. Responsibly restricting access to food and dens is a good start.

CITY SLICKERS

Any gap or opening in a building is an invitation to the resourceful raccoon. To help control raccoon populations, humans should "raccoon-proof" their living spaces and food supplies.